Citizenship

Making Friends

Cassie Mayer

Curious Fox

Curious Fox is an imprint of Capstone Global Library Limited, 7 Pilgrim Street, London, EC4V 6LB – Registered company number: 6695582

www.curious-fox.com

Editorial: Cassie Mayer and Charlotte Guillain
Design: Joanna Hinton-Malivoire
Illustrated by Mark Beech
Art editor: Ruth Blair

ISBN 978 1 782 02299 2
18 17 16
10 9 8 7 6 5 4 3

A CIP catalogue for this book is available from the British Library.

Printed and bound in China by Golden Cup Printing Co. , Ltd

Contents

A friend is someone you can trust.

Friends have fun together.

You can make friends by ...

asking someone to play with you.

You can make friends by ...

telling someone you like them.

Good friends help each other.

Good friends care for each other.

A good friend ...

takes turns choosing a game.

A good friend ...

shares her things.

A good friend ...

listens to his friends.

A good friend ...

says sorry when she is wrong.

It is important to be a good friend.

How can you be a good friend?

Activity

How is this boy being a good friend?

Picture glossary

share to let someone else use what you have; to give someone else a part of what you have

take turns give each person a chance to play something

Index